ADVENTURES OF HUEY THE HELICOPTER
FIREFIGHTING WITH FRIENDS

WRITTEN BY
CHARLIE WILSON JR

ILLUSTRATED BY
NADIA RONQUILLO

Adventures of Huey the Helicopter: Firefighting with Friends
© 2022 by Charles F. Wilson Jr.

Written by Charles F. Wilson Jr.
Illustrated by Nadia Ronquillo
Edited by John Matthew Fox of Bookfox

All rights reserved. No part of this publication may be reproduced, stored in a retrieval system, or transmitted by any means electronic, mechanical, photocopy, or recording in any form - except for brief quotations in printed reviews without prior permission from the author.

This is a work of fiction. Names, characters, places, and incidents are products of the author's imagination or are used fictitiously and are not to be construed as real. Any resemblance to actual events, locales, organizations, or persons, living or dead, is entirely coincidental. While all attempts have been made to verify the information provided in this publication, neither the author nor the publisher assumes any responsibility for errors, omissions, or contrary interpretations of the subject matter herein. Interpretation and application are the sole responsibility of the purchaser or reader. The advice and strategies found within may not be suitable for every situation. This work is sold with the understanding that neither the author nor the publisher is held responsible for the results accrued from the advice in this book. You should consult with a health professional for further details and further actions.

ISBN: 978-0-578-28438-5

FOR MY NIECE, RUMOUR.
AN ADVENTURE AWAITS.

Rumour and her kitten, Ted, dashed to wake up Huey the Helicopter.

"Huey, wake up!
The firefighters need our help!"
exclaimed Rumour, as she opened the large hangar doors.
"Smoke is coming from a nearby farm."

Huey opened his eyes but didn't move.
"Rumour, I haven't worked as a firefighter in years. I don't have what it takes anymore. Maybe one of the bigger helicopters can do the job?"

"**No way, Huey!**" Rumour said, "**We've heard stories of all the fires you used to put out back in the day. Plus, all the other helicopters are busy. It's all up to you!**" The black cat jumped on the back of the helicopter, "**Besides, our team can't have two scaredy cats,**" Ted said "**That's my job!**"

The helicopter slowly lowered the big bucket into the water.
"It's too heavy, team! I don't think I can do it."
Huey shuddered and nearly fell into the lake.

Rumour and Ted began to chant.
"Lift Huey, lift. Lift, Huey, lift!"

Ted climbed on top of Rumour's head,
"**Don't let me get wet, Huey!
Use max power!**"

With greater confidence, Huey lifted with all his might.
"**Hold on team, I can do this!**"

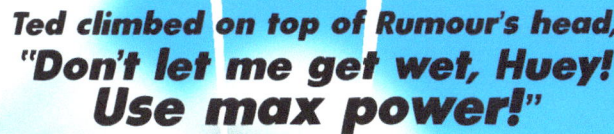

The helicopter lifted into the air and the big bucket leapt out of the water. "Way to go, Huey! We knew you could do it," cheered Rumour.

"Well, I had a few doubts," Ted said. "But I'm so glad I didn't have to go for a swim."

Rumour ran to the barn and opened the door, "Come on Mrs. Moo! We have to get you out of here!"

The helicopter wiggled its long tail and the bucket's door broke free.

"Look out below!" shouted Huey.

The water splashed over the barn and extinguished the fire.

"I've earned that cat nap now," yawned Ted. "Don't let any roosters wake me up." Huey and Rumour laughed, as the team flew home into the beautiful sunset.

CPSIA information can be obtained
at www.ICGtesting.com
Printed in the USA
LVHW070831060523
746302LV00007B/43